Illustrated By Perla Jones

Edited by Tifa Mkwawa

Marie chose a book theme surrounding learning disabilities for both personal and professional reasons. Her struggle with overcoming the daily challenges with her learning disability, known as Auditory Perception, and learning ways to overcome those challenges inspired her to write her first book during her college years.

Her professional reasons for writing this story back in 1989 were simple. At first, she did not see many books addressing this topic on bookshelves. Other motives include defining what each learning disability is and providing a clear label for it. Second, Marie disliked the way the children were treated by both their classmates and teachers. Third, she wanted to help children (with or without disability) learn to overcome their challenges. For example, to help other children understand how to be friends with a unique group of children and how to interact with them. Lastly, she also wants to encourage children to make better choices and provide alternatives instead of acting out.

She is hoping that this book will ultimately become a book series, which is meant to be a teaching point on acceptance and a teaching tool. Bubble Bear's Special Problem, focusing on Dyslexia, is just the beginning. Future books will address learning disabilities such as - Dyscalculia (math), ADHD, Auditory Perception, Attention-Deficit/Hyperactivity Disorder, and Autism. The purpose of each book is to view struggles and victories through the lens of the child. To understand someone, you need to know what they experience and learn how to help them. Releasing this book is her 30 – year dream.

To Heidi, Deborah, Mark Hunter, Latifa (Tifa) Mkwawa, Loreal Lee, Regina Robinson, Georgia Varjas, Tawnya Sutherland, Karen Skehel and Thornton Sully for providing support and encouragement during my book launch.

My sincere appreciation to Tifa for her exceptional proofreading skills, Mark and Tawnya for their support and encouragement throughout this process and journey. A special thank you goes to Mario Cuarez, Leah Lozano, Heidi, Loreal Lee, Perla Jones, Vincent Adeosun, who helped make my book a reality. Your contribution has helped my 30-year dream come to existence.

To my childhood friend, Tim, thank you for always being a good friend to me growing up and helping me get over the fears of growing up with a learning disability. We are finally sharing stories like Bubble Bear's, to reveal the untold stories of the struggles and victories that children with learning disabilities experience daily.
I am excited to share more books with you about learning disabilities soon, I know you are.

WHAT DIFFERENT PEOPLE HAVE TO SAY ABOUT THE BOOK

"I am so glad to see that she has taken the Time to tackle the challenges linked to learning disabilities in an easy-to-understand format for children. It is so important for all kids, no matter their ability level, to feel they have a place in the world."
Perfect Prose Proofreading, Heidi M.

"Bubble Bear's Special Problem' is the kind of book that will provide comfort, confidence, and acceptance to children who often feel they are different from their classmates.
Expert Marketing Ninja, Deborah D.

"Bubble Bear is a clear example of how the children of today can thrive with proper care. As someone who struggled through my k12 school years, I can relate to the different learning modalities."
Mark of Approval Web & Marketing, Mark Hunter

I have reviewed the book and shared my comments. In the beginning, you have a slide explaining why you are writing this book and the future of other books. I think this is well done and it establishes expectations of the parent, teacher, or other readers. Overall, this is great work and effort. Thanks again for letting me look over this effort. Good luck in getting this published and marketed to schools. This is a great idea and is needed in society.
Respectfully, Mike Hoskin, Retired from the Army as a General Officer

"I read your story several times, and read up on dyslexia to help me understand how I might help you achieve your goal. This looks fine and is certainly a contribution towards solving a problem, helping to destigmatize dyslexia. Well done! Thank you again for allowing me to participate however slightly in the development of this most worthwhile project. Best wishes from Europe."
Thornton Sully, Editor-in-chief

This is Bubble Bear.

His classmates are Clara Bear, Mary Bear, Bo Bear, Brainy Bear, and Luke Bear.

They have a large school named Brown Bear School.
Its students and teachers come from the forest, the
fields, the lakes, and the mountains.

This is Bubble Bear's first-grade classroom. The first grade has six different teachers. Bubble Bear's teacher's name is Miss Brown. They also have a gym teacher and someone called a special teacher who tutors children with learning problems.

At the assembly, Miss Brown calls attendance to make
sure all the students are at school. Next, they say the
Pledge of Allegiance to the flag.

"We need to add a number to our calendar and talk about what we are going to do today," said Miss Brown.

Miss Brown said, "We are going to have a math worksheet, a reading exercise, and a spelling worksheet this morning. Then, this afternoon, we will have a science test, work on our art projects, and have a music lesson."

"Write down the first addition problem and answer it." "Okay!" the class responded.

"Bubble Bear, What is the answer to two plus one? Asked Ms. Brown asked."asked, Miss Brown. Bubble Bear answered, "It equals 3.

"Miss Brown said, "That is correct! Now for homework, I would like everyone to finish page 65."

"Next, please pull out your reading books and turn to the title page. Bubble Bear, please read the title of today's story," asked Miss Brown. "The-Lost-Bog," Bubble Bear tried. "Not quite it," Miss Brown corrected. "Brainy Bear, please tell us the title," asked Miss Brown. "The Lost Dog' is today's title," snickered Brainy Bear.

Then Brainy Bear and Bubble Bear exchange mean looks because Bubble Bear got the title of the book wrong. "That is correct Brainy Bear; you get to read the story today," commented Miss Brown. When Bubble Bear reads the title of the book wrong, he gets mad and throws it on the ground. "Bubble Bear, please pick up the book and put it on your desk." requested Miss Brown.

The story was about a dog who was lost in the city and could't find his way back home to his family in the country.
Miss Brown had asked us to draw our favorite scene. I drew the scene where the dog couldn't read the stop sign. Now we must do a spelling worksheet. I'm not fond of spelling.

After the reading corner, Bubble Bear thinks to himself:
Indoor free play is my idea of fun. I like to read and play games
with my friends, and sometimes by myself.
He sees his friends are playing games and they ask him,
"Bubble Bear, do you want to play Monopoly with us?" Bubble
Bear responds by pointing the book at them and the teacher
sees him.
"Bubble Bear, don't use that book like a gun." Miss Brown
called out.

Miss Brown said to the class, "The letters A-a, B-b, and C-c are printed on the worksheet I am going to hand out. There are pictures next to each letter. Write the name of each picture on the line next to the picture." "Okay!" the class responded.

Miss Brown announced, "Time for lunch. Would you please put the papers on my desk and line up to go to the bathroom? Then, come in, get your lunch boxes and sit at your desks." "Bubble Bear, please go wipe up the milk you spilled," requested Miss Brown.

She then said, "it's time to line up for the bathroom, and then we go out to recess. Bubble Bear, don't hit Clara Bear. Please apologize to her and go to the back of the line." "Line up it's time for recess," announced Miss Brown. *I love recess, thought Bubble Bear to himself.*

At outdoor recess, Bubble Bear comes and punches Brainy Bear on the chest, and gets mad and storms off.

"Bubble Bear get down from the tree and apologize to Brainy Bear," requested Miss Brown.

After recess, everyone comes into the classroom to take the science test.

I like science, but I wouldn't say I like tests, Bubble Bear thought to himself during the science test.

After the test, Miss Brown announced to the class, "Go find your art projects and start working on them. I like the colors you used in your painting, Bubble Bear."

Later she asked the class to line up to get water and come back to the rug for music. "Today, we are going to sing Baby Beluga," announced Miss Brown.
"Good singing voices," she complimented the class. "All right, everyone, time to get ready and line up to go home," she said afterwards.

"Bubble Bear, I called your parents, and they are coming to get you; please get ready and sit on the rug," said Miss Brown.

"Mr. and Mrs. Bear, I need to talk to you about Bubble Bear. But, first, let me start by saying that Bubble Bear is talented in art, math, and music," said Miss Brown.

"I got concerned when I noticed him acting up in class all day. It is April, and he still has trouble reading but is doing better than in September. I think Bubble Bear has a special problem with learning," she added. "I noticed when I asked Bubble Bear to read the word 'dog' in the title of book, he answered it with the word 'bog'. I suspect that Bubble Bear's special reading problem is called Dyslexia," she explained further.

Mr. and Mrs. Bear asked, "What is the definition of Dyslexia?" Miss Brown answered, "Dyslexia means having trouble learning to read or interpret words or letters. Let me explain the cause of Dyslexia. First of all, experts cannot agree on one cause of the condition."

"Second, a notable scientist, called a neurologist, thinks that a person with Dyslexia sees letters and words differently. Other experts feel that it could be inherited from someone in the family, plus many other possibilities. I also took note of his spelling test, which was fine except he reversed his letters," added Miss Brown.

"Bubble Bear learns differently than his classmates and does have a lot to offer our class. One of the principles we teach is that acceptance is a choice. We believe in accepting the unique talents that our students bring to our classroom," said Miss Brown.

"Is there a solution to help Bubble Bear with his reading?"
Momma Bear wanted to know. Miss Brown said, "We can help
him by letting Bubble Bear go to the special tutor, called a
Reading Specialist. I can also assist by talking to his classmates
about his problem."

Miss Brown explained the steps the school would take to help Bubble Bear. "The special tutor would look at his work and my observations. Then, she will be observing and working with him on his learning problem. Finally, she will send a copy of the written report to you. Is that alright with you?" Miss Brown asked. Mr. and Mrs. Bear nodded, 'yes.'

Mr. and Mrs. Bear turned and said to Bubble Bear, "We love you for who you are, and we are going to help you in any way we can. But you will have to work twice as hard as the rest of your friends to be as successful. Will you do that?"

"I will," agreed Bubble Bear. Bubble Bear agreed to try, and he felt better now that he knew about his challenge with learning and that other people did too. He liked that his parents loved him anyway despite his special learning problem. This made Bubble Bear feel happy inside as he smiled and waved goodbye to Miss Brown.

Bubble Bear said. "See you tomorrow Miss Brown."
"See you tomorrow Bubble Bear," responded Miss Brown.

THE END

Matching Game

LITERACY

NAME:

DATE: :

This is how dyslexic children view words.

Draw a line to match the misspelled word to the correct word.

Dall	Ball
Dry	Bry
BOG	Dat
Bat	DOG

Glossary of Terms
For Bubble Bear's Special Problem

Recess- This is your break time.

Choice- Choosing between two or more things.

Dyslexia - This is when you have trouble learning to read or interpret words or letters.

Tutors - Teachers that are there to help you learn a subject in a smaller group.

Apologize – Saying sorry from the heart when you do something wrong.

Neurologist - A doctor that studies your nerves.